Love Omar

Hannah Khalil

methuen | drama

LONDON • NEW YORK • OXFORD • NEW DELHI • SYDNEY

METHUEN DRAMA
Bloomsbury Publishing Plc, 50 Bedford Square, London, WC1B 3DP, UK
Bloomsbury Publishing Inc, 1359 Broadway, New York, NY 10018, USA
Bloomsbury Publishing Ireland, 29 Earlsfort Terrace, Dublin 2, D02 AY28, Ireland

BLOOMSBURY, METHUEN DRAMA and the Methuen Drama logo are trademarks of Bloomsbury Publishing Plc

First published in Great Britain 2026

Cover design: Debs King
Cover image: Omar Sharif © INTERFOTO via Alamy, photo frame border © Michele via Adobe Stock

A catalogue record for this book is available from the British Library.

A catalog record for this book is available from the Library of Congress.

ISBN: PB: 978-1-3506-6162-2
ePDF: 978-1-3506-6163-9
eBook: 978-1-3506-6164-6

Series: Modern Plays

Typeset by Westchester Publishing Services

For product safety related questions contact productsafety@bloomsbury.com.

To find out more about our authors and books visit www.bloomsbury.com and sign up for our newsletters.

Love Omar was originally commissioned by Chichester Festival Theatre. It was produced by Theatro Technis and premiered on 13 May, 2026.

The cast was as follows:

(in order of appearance)

Daphne	**Ishia Bennison**
Omar	**Al Nedjari**
Mag	**Lara Sawalha**

CREATIVES

Writer	**Hannah Khalil**
Director	**Chris White**
Set & Costume Designer	**Pip Terry**
Lighting Designer	**Marty Langthorne**
Composer & Sound Designer	**Michael Picknett**
Movement Director	**John Nicholson**
Casting Director	**Hannah Miller, CDG**
Publicist	**Nancy Poole**
Production Manager	**Thomas Quine**
Company Stage Manager	**Abi Morris**
Assistant Stage Manager	**Evie Rostant**
Costume Supervisor	**Petros Kourtellaris**
Poster Design	**Debs King**
Arabic Consultants	**Lara Sawalha, Hassan Abdulrazzak and Ghareeb Iskander**
Producer	**Laila Alj**

This text may differ slightly from the play as performed

Ishia Bennison (Daphne)

Ishia trained at Manchester Polytechnic, and has recently been seen at the RSC and on film as the Nurse in *Romeo and Juliet*, and on TV as Joyce in *Happy Valley*.

Theatre credits include: *Three Sisters* and *Measure for Measure* (Shakespeare's Globe); *The Tempest*, *Romeo and Juliet*, *Merry Wives of Windsor*, *Mad World My Masters*, *Candide*, *A New Way to Please You*, *Sejanus – His Fall*, *Speaking Like Magpies*, *Cymbeline* and *Measure for Measure* (Royal Shakespeare Company); *Goats* and *Our Private Life* (Royal Court); *Half Life* (Ustinov, Bath); *Julius Caesar* – all female (Donmar); *The Importance of Being Earnest* (The Rose, Hong Kong Festival); *The Canterbury Tales* (tour and The Rose); *Strange Orchestra* and *Mother Courage* (Orange Tree); *Who's Afraid of Virginia Woolf?* (Manchester Library); *Antony and Cleopatra* (BAM, New York); *A Midsummer Night's Dream* (Brazil tour); *Merry Wives* (India tour); *Richard III* (Riverside Studios / The Tower of London); *Samson Agonistes* and *Romeo and* Juliet (Northern Broadsides); *Medea* (Lilian Baylis); *Les Misérables* (Nottingham Playhouse).

TV credits include: *Happy Valley*, *New Tricks*, *Last Tango in Halifax*, *True Dare Kiss*, *Holby City* and *EastEnders* (BBC); *At Home with the Braithwaites*, *Emmerdale* and *Coronation Street* (ITV).

Film credits include: *Much Ado About Nothing* (BBC), *King David* (Paramount Pictures), *Jesus of Nazareth* (ITC Entertainment).

Al Nedjari (Omar)

Al has been an actor for nearly thirty years.

Having trained at the Poor School in London, his first acting role was as a regular in the British soap opera, *Coronation Street*.

Early in his career, Al worked with writer and director, Stephen Berkoff, and went on to develop a specialism in physical theatre. This culminated in the founding of theatre company, Gecko, with whom Al created and performed in four shows, appearing at theatre festivals throughout the world. More recently, he was a movement artist in the Oscar-winning space movie, *Gravity*, starring Sandra Bullock and George Clooney. Al has performed regularly at the National Theatre in London, most recently in *My Brilliant Friend*, an adaptation of the novels by Elena Ferranti. Having performed in the hugely successful *War Horse* at both the National Theatre and in the West End, he then movement directed BBC Prom 22 'The War Horse Prom', at the Royal Albert Hall.

Al can be seen on Netflix, in each of the first three seasons of *Bridgerton*, and in the British horror movie, *The Strays*. He has performed alongside Woody Harrelson in the film, *Lost in London*, notable because it was transmitted live into cinemas as it was being shot.

Lara Sawalha (Mag)

Theatre credits include: *The Ministry of Lesbian Affairs* (Soho Theatre); *Connect Now* (The Old Vic); *The Abyss* (Royal Court Theatre and Edinburgh Festival); *Why It's Kicking Off Everywhere* (Young Vic); *Oil* (Almeida Theatre); *Another World* (National Theatre); *A Is for Ali* (The Old Red Lion); and *Nahda* (Bush Theatre).

Television credits include: *FBI: International*; *Casualty* and *Doctors*.

Film credits include: *Roads to Olympia*; *45 Minutes to Ramallah*; *The Last Friday* and *High Heels.*

Lara is a highly experienced voice artist and some of her most notable credits include: *Final Fantasy XVI*, *Cyberpunk 2077* and *Assassin's Creed*. She was also nominated for best actress in the BBC Audio awards for the portrayal of Selma in the *Yafa Cherry Orchard* radio play

CREATIVES

Hannah Khalil (Writer)

Hannah Khalil is Writer in Residence at Bristol Old Vic (2025–30). Recent work includes critically acclaimed *My English Persian Kitchen*, which had a sell-out run at the Traverse as part of the Edinburgh Festival Fringe in August 2024, and then transferred to Soho Theatre, London. It returned to London in autumn 2025 followed by a UK and Irish tour.

Hannah was the 2022 Resident Writer at Shakespeare's Globe, while there the Globe produced three of her plays: *Hakawatis: Women of the Arabian Nights*, *Henry VIII* and *The Fir Tree* (2021 and 2022). Hannah's other stage plays include *A Museum in Baghdad* (Royal Shakespeare Company), which marked the first play by a woman of Arab heritage on a main stage at the RSC, *Interference* (National Theatre of Scotland) and the critically acclaimed *Scenes from 68* Years*, shortlisted for the James Tait Black Award (Arcola Theatre, London, 2016). Hannah is a Fellow of the Royal Society of Literature and an Associate Artist of Shakespeare's Globe.

Chris White (Director)

Chris White is a dramaturg and director specialising in international collaborations, Shakespeare, new plays, and projects with young people. He is Associate Dramaturg for Paines Plough and an Associate Learning Practitioner for The Royal Shakespeare Company, for whom he leads projects and performances across the UK and internationally; including *The Wood of Words: In Every Leaf*, which he co-wrote and directed for the 2023 RSC Playmaking Festival. His most recent production is *My English Persian Kitchen* by Hannah Khalil, which sold out at The Traverse Theatre as part of their Edinburgh Festival Fringe 2024 programme, and returned to Soho Theatre in autumn 2025 before a short UK and Irish tour.

For Soho Theatre he co-led Writer's Lab for ten years, developing plays by the UK's best emerging playwrights, as well as directing Soho Theatre Young Playwrights Festival. Other productions of new work in the UK include *Chippy* (Acorn Theatre, Penzance and Cornwall tour); *The Lighthouse Keeper's Son* (Samuel Beckett Research Centre, Reading University); *Nothing in a Butterfly* (Synergy Theatre/Omnibus); *Gutted* (Marlowe Theatre, Canterbury and UK tour); *Trouble and Wonder* (RSC); *Booby's Bay* (London/Bristol/Cornwall); *bottled* (VAULT Festival); *Scenes from 68* Years* (Arcola Theatre); *The Sale* (Chapter Arts, Cardiff); and *The Water When It Burns* (Hampstead Theatre).

International productions include: *The Truth* (La Virgule, Lille); *Fewer Emergencies* (Teatro Litta, Milan); *Hard Places* (Prithvi Theatre, Mumbai and national tour); *The Suicide* (Teatro Della Contraddizione, Milan); and *A Midsummer Night's Dream* (National Centre for Performing Arts, Beijing, currently touring across China). His production of *Trouf*, co-directed in Tunisia in 2019 for Nabeul Performing Arts Centre, premiered in the UK as part of the 2023 Shubbak Festival and was funded by the British Council.

Pip Terry (Set & Costume Design)

Pip graduated from Wimbledon College of Art with a degree in Theatre Design in 2020. She won the Linbury Prize for Stage Design in 2021 and worked as the Kiln Theatre's Resident Assistant Designer throughout 2022.

She has since worked as a model maker and design assistant on a number of productions, including *My Master Builder* (Wyndham's Theatre); *The Other Place* (National Theatre); and *The Lady from the Sea* (The Bridge Theatre).

Pip has worked as a design associate supporting shows such as *The Time Traveller's Wife* (Apollo Theatre); *Once on this Island* (Regent's Park Open Air Theatre); and *Hamnet* (RSC) as well as designing the set and costumes for several of her own shows, including *My English Persian Kitchen* (Soho Theatre); *The Shivers* (New Diorama Theatre, Polka Theatre); and a variety of touring shows including *The Sex Education Musical* (UK schools).

As a scenic artist, Pip's credits include Disney's *Frozen* (Theatre Royal Drury Lane); *Moulin Rouge!* (Piccadilly Theatre); and *Cabaret* (the Kit Kat Club).

Marty Langthorne (Lighting Design)

Marty Langthorne is a London-based artist and lighting designer whose work encompasses live art, theatre, performance, dance and fine art.

Recent credits: *Feral Monster* (National Theatre of Wales); *Zoetrope* and *Mabon* (National Dance Company of Wales); *Showmanism* and *Remember Me* by Dickie Beau (Hamsptead Theatre); *It's Come to This* by Meow Meow (Soho Theatre); *When the World Turns* (Oily Cart); *Nice Things* (Pleasance); *Shooting from Below* by Midgitte Bardot (Southbank Centre); *In the Heart of the Nest* (Luxembourg Philharmonie).

Previous collaborations with Chris White include *My English Persian Kitchen* (Soho Theatre); *Nothing in a Butterfly* (Omnibus); *Gutted* (Marlowe Theatre); *Scenes from 68 Years* (Arcola Theatre); *Bottled* (VAULT Festival).

He is co-creator of First Light, an immersive installation of light and sound for babies and their families.

As Part of the Duckie Collective, he has designed many of their theatrical club events.

As a light artist he creates installations investigating human response to colour in the natural world.

Michael Picknett (Sound Design & Composition)

Originally trained as a composer, Michael Picknett is equally at home in the theatrical tech box as on the concert stage. He is a musician, sound designer, touring technical manager and academic specialising in devising techniques. He works mainly in contemporary dance and film, between the UK and the EU. As a sound designer, he specialises in creating immersive sound music for live performance – often using custom designed multi-speaker set-ups, and live manipulation of sound.

John Nicholson (Movement Direction)

John is the Artistic Director of Peepolykus. Eight of his plays are published.

As writer: *A Trespasser's Guide to the Classics*, *Rik Mayall's Bedside Tales* series 1 and 2, *Baskervilles*, *Marley Was Dead* (BBC Radio 4); *The Time Machine* (Olivier nominated – 2024); *Hound of the Baskervilles* (West End, Duchess); *No Wise Men* (Liverpool Playhouse); *King Arthur* (Bristol Old Vic); *Madame Bovary* (Jermyn Street Theatre); *Spyski* (Lyric Hammersmith); *The Ramsbury Players* (National Theatre); *Richard's Rampage* (Old Vic, London); *Arthur Conan Doyle's Appreciation Society* (Edinburgh Traverse).

As comedy consultant: *One Man, Two Guvnors* (Bolton Octagon); *A Little Hotel on the Side* (Theatre Royal Bath); *Watson and Oliver* and *The Wrong Door* (BBC); *Accidental Death of an Anarchist* (West End); *Black Comedy* (Orange Tree); *Three Men in a Boat* (Rose Theatre, Kingston).

As director: *Tweedy's Massive Circus* (RSC); *Baskervilles* (Theatre by the Lake); *Partners in Crime* (Queens Theatre); *Dracula – the Bloody Truth* (Plymouth Theatre Royal); *Shaun the Sheep Live* (Aardman); *Nina Conti* and *Paul Merton* (West End); *Spymonkey's Spookshow* (Blackpool Winter Gardens); *The Light Princess* (Tobacco Factory, Bristol); *A Christmas Carol* (Exeter Northcott).

Thomas Quine (Production Manager)

Thomas J. Quine is a production manager for theatre and events.

Recent Production Management credits include: *Slippery* (Omnibus Theatre); *Anne of Green Gables* and *NEZHA* (Emma Wang Productions Ltd.); *Before the Millennium* (Old Fire Station Oxford); *Sense & Sensibility* and *Theo In Between* (British Youth Music Theatre); *Tuck Everlasting* (National Youth Music Theatre); *The Jungle Book* (Wiltshire Creative); *Unfiltered* (Pentabus); *NOSTOS*, *The Gel*, *Table* and *Callisto* (Oxford School of Drama); *Even More Ghost Stories by Candlelight* (UK tour, MAKE ME- Workshop HighTide Theatre); *L'Incoronazione di Poppea* and *La Cenerentola* (Hampstead Garden Opera); *On|Off Presents the Disruptors* (London Fashion Week 2025); *Homo Alone* (The Other Palace); *Snakes and Ladders* (Oxford School of Drama); *Dahling You Were Marvellous*, *Lemons Lemons Lemons Lemons Lemons*, *Pool (no water)*, *Afterlife* (RCSSD); *Shrek*, *Loserville* and *Carrie* (all University of Chichester); *DogShit* (Theatre503),

Recent Assistant / Associate Credits include: *The Code* (Deus Ex Machina); *Macbeth* (Dukes Theatre Company); *Cavalleria Rusticana* (Blackheath Halls); *Into the Woods* and *Spring Awakening* (Royal Academy of Music); *The Dream of a Ridiculous Man* and *The Dry House* (Marylebone Theatre); *On|Off Presents Jack Irving* (London Fashion Week 2024).

Hannah Miller, CDG (Casting Director)

Hannah was the RSC's Head of Casting from 2008 to 2022. Previously she worked as the Casting Assistant at the National Theatre (1998–2002), Deputy Head of Casting at the RSC (2003–5) and Casting Director for Birmingham Rep (2005–8).

She now works as a freelance casting director most recently working for the Royal Exchange Theatre, Manchester on productions of *Great Expectations* and *Brief Encounter*, and *My Neighbour Totoro* for the RSC. Later this year she will be working with Wales Millenium Centre on a stage adaptation of *Pontypool*. Hannah works with drama schools and industry organisations, advising actors on professional development and demystifying casting and directed the ArtsEd Actors final year showcase in both 2023 and 2024. She continues to work with the RSC's Creative Learning and Engagement team as an Associate Learning Practitioner and NextGeneration:Act champion, is a former Trustee of both Northampton Theatres Trust and Tamasha, a fellow of the RSA and an RSC Associate Artist.

THEATRO TECHNIS COMPANY LIMITED

Founded in 1957 by George Eugeniou and a group of actors, Theatro Technis began its work in an old, unused warehouse tucked behind King's Cross. What started as a modest and resourceful initiative quickly grew into a pioneering cultural organisation, shaped by determination, artistic ambition, and a strong sense of social purpose. The early years were not without difficulty, as the company navigated limited resources and the challenge of establishing an independent voice within the UK theatre landscape. Yet its commitment to accessible, socially engaged work allowed it to endure and evolve.

By the early 1960s, it had already distinguished itself as one of the first venues in the UK dedicated to serving its local, working-class, and immigrant communities—audiences whose stories were often overlooked on mainstream stages. This ethos of inclusivity and representation has remained central to the organisation's identity.

In 1974, after years of perseverance, Theatro Technis secured its permanent home in a converted church building at 26 Crowndale Road, a move that marked a significant turning point in its development. From this space, it flourished into a vibrant centre of multi-faceted and multicultural activity.

Over the decades, Theatro Technis has continued to provide a platform for international companies and independent artists, supporting new writing, experimental performance, and cross-cultural collaboration. Its programming reflects a wide range of perspectives, maintaining a strong connection to its founding mission while responding to the evolving cultural landscape. The theatre has built a reputation as a space for bold, socially conscious work that challenges audiences and amplifies underrepresented voices.

In 2022, Kerry Kyriacos Michael MBE joined as Creative Director, ushering in a new chapter for the organisation. Known for his leadership at Theatre Royal Stratford East and his commitment to culturally diverse and disruptive work, he brings renewed energy and a forward-looking vision. His approach builds on the theatre's legacy while expanding its reach and relevance for contemporary audiences. Under his leadership, Theatro Technis continues to champion independent voices and innovative storytelling.

Looking ahead, Theatro Technis has announced plans for an ambitious capital redevelopment project, estimated at £20 million. This transformation aims to strengthen the organisation's financial resilience while significantly enhancing its artistic capacity and community impact. Initial funding has already been secured, with further support to be sought from donors and partners.

Located just a ten-minute walk from King's Cross, the theatre sits at the heart of one of central London's most dynamic development areas. Working in partnership with Camden Council, the redevelopment will reimagine the existing site into a modern, accessible, and sustainable cultural hub. The project is being designed by James Houston of Wild Architects, ensuring a thoughtful and innovative approach.

Central to this vision is the ambition to establish Theatro Technis as a leading Cypriot cultural centre in London, serving a UK Cypriot community of around 450,000 people, as well as a global diaspora of approximately 1.2 million. At the same time, the theatre will continue to showcase bold work from across the Global Majority, reinforcing its longstanding commitment to diversity and inclusion.

The redevelopment will significantly expand the theatre's facilities. The main auditorium will increase from 120 to 250 seats, enabling a broader range of productions, including those incorporating live translation to reach wider audiences. Two additional performance spaces will also be created: a 90-seat basement cabaret and music venue, and a flexible studio theatre on the first floor for rehearsals, workshops, screenings, and a digital archive of Cypriot creative work.

Community engagement remains central to the project. New purpose-built spaces will support classes, workshops, social events, and residencies for local residents and artists. A public foyer with a kitchen and bar will provide a welcoming space open throughout the day, encouraging greater interaction between the theatre and its community.

Sustainability is a key priority, with the building designed around low-carbon energy solutions and urban greening initiatives that promote biodiversity and long term environmental resilience. The upper levels will include serviced apartments for visiting artists, supporting international collaboration while generating sustainable income.

Subject to planning permission, construction is expected to begin in 2027. This ambitious redevelopment marks a major step forward, ensuring that Theatro Technis continues to thrive as a vital cultural institution, honouring its past while embracing the future.

Creative Director Kerry Kyriacos Michael MBE
Producer Laila Alj
Theatre Manager Leo Clasen
Community Engagement Manager Annie Sanger Davies
Technical Manager Simon Beyer
Bookkeeper Elena Caporilli

Front of House team Angie Servan Mercatali, Connor Rowlett, Dela Ruth Hini, Eva Ceroni Marti, Matt Blaney, Mio Lobban, Robin Du Four, Sebastian Lee, Sameer Phatak, Ufuk Öncel Camcı, Anastasia Sidorova, Danny Hughes, Ella Blackburn, Megan Earl, Megan Watson, Tash Cordeaux, Riz Meedin, Eoin Sweeney, Joshua Griffin, Manasi Gokhale

Board of Directors
Dr Marilyn Panayi – Chair
Aris Eugeniou
Christos Araclides
Costas Louis
Lucy Christy
Michael Constantine
Panos Savvides
Steve Constantine
Dorota Krimmel

Creative Partners

The Production Exchange
A charity whose objective is to support, mentor and offer opportunity to as many Creative Artists from as widely diverse a catchment as possible.

The London Sinfonietta
One of the world's finest contemporary music ensembles with a reputation built on cutting-edge programming and virtuosic performances.

Scene & Heard
A unique project partnering inner-city children of Somers Town with theatre professionals.

Realfake Theatre
A performance duo by Nina Bowers and Philip Arditti. They make and tour entertaining and thought-provoking theatre.

Kyriacos And Company
An independent production company working in the live and recorded arts

Associate Artists

Ché Walker
Evan Reynolds (Trainee associate)
Eve Polycarpou
Jack Mckee (Trainee associate)
Martha D Lewis
Mukhtar Moalin (Trainee associate)
Nina Bowers
Philip Arditti
Sophia Vi
Uchenna Ngwe
Vic Holt (Trainee associate)

Friends and Patrons

Here at Theatro Technis, we are dedicated to showcasing unheard voices and those with an independent mind and spirit. As a Charity with no regular funding, our work can only succeed with the support of those listed below. We are grateful for their unwavering support, including our Honorary Patrons, whom we have identified as going above and beyond in their support over the years.

Join as a friend and patron here:

Founding Patron

GEORGE EUGENIOU
MAROULA EUGENIOU

Partners

Camden Council
The High Commission of Cyprus in the UK

Big Gift

Dawn and Ira Smalberg
Dr Marilyn Panayi
Dynamis Ltd
Marsh family
Marcus Markou
Rebecca and John Gibbs
The Theatre Trust

Legacy Gift

Murray Melvin
Philip Hedley

Special Patron

Peter Kosta

Patron
Fusari Laura
Kerry Kyriacos Michael
Panos Savvides

Friend
David Byrne
Dominic & Shelley Barody
Dorota Krimmel
Edward Forman
Keiko Mizuno
Lesley Symons
Martin Fisher FRSA
Rosalie Carn
Tim Poole
And all those who wish to stay anonymous

THEATRO TECHNIS,
26 Crowndale Road,
London NW1 1TT
Company no. 01509049,
Charity no. 280885, VAT no. 736113455.
An Independent Theatre Council member

Love Omar

Hannah Khalil

Characters

Omar
Mag
Daphne the Dresser

This play is a work of fiction, although it is inspired by actual events and people.

Pre-show the stage is empty but as the audience enter the dressing room is made. We hear the radio and the newsreader throughout this process. Gradually we are backstage. A dressing room. September 1983. Pre-show. It's messy. Make-up. Overflowing ashtray. Several-day-old flowers in a vase. A phone on the wall. A backgammon board on a side table. Several packs of cards. A copy of Othello *in sight.*

The radio is on. It plays either 'Blue Monday' by New Order or 'This Is Not a Love Song' by Public Image Ltd or something else to locate us in 1983. At the end of the song the DJ introduces the news:

Newsreader This is the six o'clock news – Joan Halroyd reporting. This evening's main stories:

The United States has accused the USSR of shooting down a civilian airliner which is missing off Russia's eastern coast. All 269 people on board the Korean Airlines flight KAL 007 are presumed dead. Moscow has so far only admitted to an incident with an 'unidentified aircraft' in Soviet airspace. The Boeing 747 was flying from the USA to Seoul via Anchorage. Elsewhere, thirty-eight prisoners have escaped from a high security prison in Northern Ireland. One prison officer has been killed and another seriously injured during the mass break-out of Republican inmates from the Maze jail near Lisburn. Ten of the prisoners were recaptured in the first few hours, but the remainder are still on the run. Security forces mounted the biggest search operation Northern Ireland has ever seen within minutes of the escape. We will bring you more on this story as it develops.

The sounds of the racing report intro music.

Radio Welcome to the racing report, today's selection: Crusader Castle in the 3.15 at Epsom –

The last item is brought in by **Daphne**. *It is a costume newly laundered and wrapped in cellophane. She hangs it on the wall and then turns back as if it has called her. She looks coyly left and right then points to herself – you're asking me to dance? She* *lifts the costume off the wall and begins to dance with it – she's getting carried away. She realises she is crushing it to her and she will crease it so stops suddenly and hangs it up again. She smooths it down. Then turns off the radio and on the show relay. She goes to the mirror to check her hair isn't dishevelled after her antics . . .*

We hear the noises in the theatre as it is being set up for the show. She looks at the almost-full ashtray and picks up one of the cigarette butts, lifting it to her lips as if to kiss it, but a noise on the relay makes her jump and she exits swiftly.

Pause.

Now **Omar** *enters – as he does the sweeping theme music from Lawrence of Arabia plays. He walks elegantly, with swagger, like a star, until . . .*

He trips over a roller boot and the music rapidly cuts out.

He is in a foul mood.

He is carrying an envelope.

He picks up the boot.

Omar Where the bloody hell is everyone!

He hears voices of actors on stage warming up – tongue twisters and the like – on the relay. He nods – aha, that's where they are – and sits down in front of the mirror still holding the roller boot. He looks at himself in the mirror and sighs in disappointment at the age he has become. He examines his greying hair – is that dandruff? – his grey eyebrows and lacklustre moustache with disappointment.

He sighs deeply.

Is there a doctor in the house? I don't even look like Omar Sharif any more.

He opens the envelope in his hand and looks at the money inside – it is his pay packet. He puts it in the drawer without much attention.

Tannoy Ladies and gentlemen of *The Sleeping Prince* company to the stage for your warm-up – *The Sleeping Prince* company to the stage for your warm-up please –

Omar (*to himself*) You know very well Mr Sharif does his own warm-up thank you.

He gets up and puts the roller boot on his chair. He begins to attempt some stretches – but his heart is not in it. So he stops and lights a cigarette.

The sheikh shakes and shivers in the light of the silvery moon, the sheikh shakes and shivers in the light of the silvery moon.

He sits down – on the roller boot.

This reignites his anger.

He holds the boot aloft.

TELL THAT CHILD NOT TO LEAVE THESE LYING AROUND – I DON'T CARE IF SHE IS PRACTISING FOR LLOYD BLOODY WEBBER SHE'LL KILL SOMEONE.

A beat.

AND WHAT THE HELL WAS SHE DOING IN MY DRESSING ROOM. IT'S MY SODDING DRESSING ROOM – NOT HERS – NOT ALAN BATES' – MINE!

He throws the rollerboot in frustration at the door where a young woman has appeared. She is **Mag**. *She ducks and the boot misses her.* **Omar** *is immediately on his feet.*

Mag WOAH!

Omar Did I hurt you?

Mag No –

Omar Come in.

Mag I think I'm safer here!

Omar (*holding up his hands*) Come in please, I'm unarmed. I promise. I never lie. Come in.

Mag *walks in uneasily, leaving the door open behind her. He goes and retrieves the boot then approaches her with ease and looks her over, encouraging her to turn in front of him.*

Omar No scratches?

Mag No. Don't worry I'm just –

Omar Are you sure?

Mag Yeah – I'm fine.

Omar Please let me make it up to you.

Mag That's not –

Omar *has picked up a phone and is dialling.*

Omar Pepita? It's me. I want to bring the company home for dinner after the show tonight. Can you manage it? (*He puts his hand over the receiver to talk to* **Mag**.) Hand them over, and you can go. (*Back to the phone –* **Mag** *looks confused.*) I know and I do love that restaurant but I don't want to be in public. I'm spending all evening being stared at on stage I'd prefer not to be stared at while I'm eating. I know I don't usually mind but not tonight. (*He puts his hand over the receiver to talk to* **Mag**.) Well? Come on, I need them. (*Back to the phone –* **Mag** *looks more confused.*) Listen if you can't rustle something up we can order food and get someone to pick it up. Aha. Yes. I thought you'd say that. Great. No not Arabic. Paella maybe? How many? I don't know – I haven't invited them yet. (*He rolls his eyes at* **Mag**.) Let's say everyone. Everyone's everyone. Cast, crew, everyone. No not the whole bloody audience – no need to be facetious. (*A beat.*) Yes, even Mrs Arnold, I can't not invite her, okay, she's my co-star? Fine. Good. Yes after the show. Thank you. (*He hangs up. To* **Mag**.) And you must come. By way of peace treaty yes?

Mag It really is very generous of you. Dinner. For everyone.

Omar Oh it's nothing. I hate to eat alone.

Mag What if they're not free?

Omar They make themselves free. For me. How often do you get to dine with a Hollywood star, eh?

A beat.

Mag So – um – all that's – thrown me. (*She gathers herself and returns to what she rehearsed.*) I wanted to congratulate you on last night, it was great.

Omar *turns down the show relay.*

Omar Thank you – very kind. Now hand them over and you can go.

Mag Hand –?

Omar The underpants.

Mag –?

Omar Knickers. Briefs. Undies.

Mag My –?

Omar Listen, I'm making a big concession here – I'd rather not wear any frankly – uncomfortable bloody things. I'm being accommodating – but if you can't get them cleaned in a timely fashion then I won't be wearing any tonight. I told Daphne – it's as simple as that.

A beat.

Mag You only have one pair of pants?

Omar You're not here about the underpants are you?

Mag No.

A beat.

Mag Oh. You don't know who I am.

Omar I recognise you. I thought you were from costume. People seem to come and go here – a never-ending conveyor belt – the only loyal one is Daphne – my dresser – where is she?

Mag I'm not from costume.

Omar But I know you don't I? I never forget a face . . . So familiar – and yet . . . Remind me.

Mag It's Mag.

Omar Like Maggie Thatch–?

Mag No. Like Mag.

A beat.

Omar *still looks blank.*

Mag Rehearsals? Boiling room? No windows that opened? Mish-mash of uncomfortable chairs. Director stood seriously. Stage managers looking nervously at the clock . . . I was the one sat in the corner. Not really allowed to speak. The AD.

Omar *looks blank.*

Mag Assistant director. That's all.

Omar Ah. So Peter sent you.

Mag Well . . . Peter is gone. On to another job. As directors do. Hang around until press night and then once the moment of glory has passed they vanish. Off to pastures new. While the rest of the team have to keep ploughing this one.

A beat.

Has she said too much?

Omar Go on.

Mag And I – as Peter's assistant – am tasked with the job of keeping the play at the standard which he left it.

A beat.

Mag So (*Back to the prepared speech.*) I just came by to say hello and congratulate you on a great performance and –

Omar And then I attacked you.

Mag *looks confused.*

Omar With the boot – Frankie's, what the hell was she doing in my dressing room anyway? Sweet girl . . . I hope you'll forgive me . . .

Mag Um – yes – forget it.

Omar Great.

He turns away from her to the mirror. She has been dismissed. When he looks up she is still there.

Omar Something else?

Mag Oh – and um I was just wanting – to – flag up those lines . . .

Omar Which lines?

Mag In the first scene . . . with the kiss.

Omar Rather good I thought.

Mag *approaches the door ready to flee.*

Mag Yes great (*A beat.*) but you, um, fluffed them a bit. Just look over them – thanks.

She's about to dash off.

Omar I didn't FLUFF anything. It was *her* fault – she paraphrased and mixed me up. Again. I sometimes wonder if she does it on purpose . . . Other than that I was word perfect last night. Word perfect.

Mag Ok. Just – if you wouldn't mind looking over them again before you go on tonight that'd be –

She's about to go.

Omar Where are you going then?

Mag To talk to the rest of the company.

Omar Who will run lines with me?

Mag I – maybe – you could ask – Daphne?

Omar Daphne is a dresser. And she's not here. You are.

He looks at **Mag**. *She is uncomfortable*

Omar There are important people in tonight you know.

A beat.

And the director wouldn't want the star to be neglected. We can run them while I do my make-up to keep Peter happy.

Mag *comes back into the room uneasily.*

Mag Um, well – actually it's the *assistant* director you've to keep happy now.

Omar I've rarely had any complaints before. In fact most women leave my company extremely happy. Buzzing. Tingling. Glowing.

A beat.

He starts preparing his make-up and getting ready. He notices **Mag** *is blushing a little.*

Omar Oh – delightful. Despite the professional exterior, it blushes. No don't be embarrassed it's good. In my country women are dependent – they blush and I like that, I'm used to that. I couldn't love a woman who couldn't or wouldn't blush.

Mag Shall we do the lines . . .

Omar Of course. (*A beat.*) As long as you're going over *her* lines too – she's no team player.

Mag And you are? (*A beat – she catches herself.*) I mean. You are the star. The lead.

Omar Even in soccer the striker has to pass the ball occasionally.

Mag Football analogies?

Omar Always been a fan – since RADA.

Mag Let me guess. Liverpool. Glory hunter.

Omar Hull City.

Mag *looks incredulous.*

Mag HULL?

Omar Blame Tom Courtenay.

A beat.

They regard each other.

Mag You are full of surprises.

A beat.

So. Let's get to these lines then I can talk to the rest of the cast.

Omar And her? You'll talk to her too?

Mag Of course.

Omar Get me my script would you? It's in the drawer over there.

Mag I thought you said you knew them.

Omar I do – I just don't want you accusing me of anything untoward . . .

Mag Like what?

Omar Paraphrasing.

Mag *goes to the drawer, opens it and takes out the script of* The Sleeping Prince *by Terence Rattigan. She takes out a backgammon set.*

Mag Checkers?

Omar Backgammon. Do you play?

Tannoy Please could someone from the stage management team come to the auditorium, we have a loose carpet that needs securing. (*Off – thinking cans are off.*) That's the third time I've asked – someone's going to break their –

Omar Take your coat off – sit down.

Mag *takes her coat off to reveal a purple jumper.* **Omar** *winces a mite.*

Omar Ah now I'm afraid you are going to have to take your sweater off too.

Mag What?

Omar I must insist.

He approaches her.

A beat.

Mag Sorry – but–

Omar OFF!

Mag I don't think – I mean – I like it on –

Omar Well I like it off.

A beat.

Off off – yulla! It's the *colour*!

Mag What's wrong with purple?

Omar Purple is the colour of Holy Week – off!

Mag SO?

Omar That's the week Christ died. Purple means death. I won't have anyone in purple anywhere near me when I'm working. It's bad luck.

Mag Oh. I never expected you to be superstitious. And . . .

Omar Yes?

Mag Never mind.

Omar Go on –

Mag Nothing.

Omar Come on. Don't be timid. It's boring. If you want to be a director you have to have balls.

A beat.

Mag Well – I just – I wondered how the world's most famous Arab knows about Holy Week?

Omar In case you've forgotten the HOLY LAND is in fair Arabia.

Mag (*sardonic*) Yeah but aren't all Arabs Muslim?

Omar No. They aren't. Now please remove your sweater.

A beat.

I must insist. What if something terrible befell me? A trip over that loose carpet – debilitated. What would the audience say if Omar Sharif couldn't go on?

A beat.

He approaches.

I can help you?

Mag No it's – fine.

She takes it off. He comes close to her and she holds her breath not knowing what he is going to do. They move closer together as though magnetised to one another as we hear the sweeping theme music from Lawrence of Arabia *– they get closer and closer until – he takes the jumper from her hands and she tries to grab it back as the music suddenly cuts out.*

Mag Hey!

Omar I'm going to throw it away.

Mag But it's mine!

Omar I don't like it.

Mag I do!

Omar My opinion is more important. You want me to be happy don't you? Making me happy is your job.

Mag No helping you get your lines right is my job.

Omar Fine and I won't be able to if you are wearing that thing.

He puts her jumper in the bin

Now tell me what Peter wants me to look at.

Mag It's not Peter it's me.

Omar Forgive me. What do you want me to look at. My assistant director.

A woman appears in the doorway with a large sack of post. It is **Daphne**, *a dresser. She is struggling.*

Daphne 'Scuse me, Mr Sharif. I didn't know you had company. (*To* **Mag**.) I think the warm-up has started, Mag.

Mag I know.

Daphne They'll need you for that.

Mag I'll go in a minute.

Daphne And Mr Sharif needs his space before the show. There's an important person in tonight.

Omar It's okay, Daphne. Where's George? (*Indicating post bag.*) That's hardly woman's work.

Daphne He's refused to deliver any more of your post.

She tries to lift the post bag and winces.

Bit of help, Mag? As you're here. Not you, Mr Sharif. Can't risk anything happening to our star. (*To* **Mag**.) On three – one – two – three.

Together they lift the bag and move it into a corner of the room.

Mag All this is for you?

Omar Why are you surprised? (*To* **Daphne**.) Is George's sciatica bad again?

Daphne No. It's his heart that's the problem. (*To* **Mag**.) Did you know stage door George had a bypass last autumn?

Mag So lifting this is bad for his heart?

Daphne No. It's the *content* that's dangerous.

Mag *approaches the sack curiously and takes out a letter. It has a picture of a woman in her underwear on the outside of the envelope.*

Mag WHOA!

Daphne Isn't it disgraceful. George says the postmaster's complained twice. Not just about the amount of letters but the fact it's distracting the sorters. Hold-ups on the line . . . All the Portsmouth, Gosport, Havant, Cosham addresses are fine but Chichester post's all delayed cos of the gawping. Backlog. That sort of thing's slowing them right down. They've never known anything like it. Not often they get an eyeful during a shift. Who are these women?

Omar Now, now, Daphne, don't be judgemental. I'll send the post office some chocolates by way of apology. And to George – remind him it's not my fault, Daphne. I don't invite this sort of thing . . .

Daphne (*produces a birthday card*) 'Course you don't, it's one of the burdens of stardom. The things you have to contend with! Oh – there's also this – for the new ASM – the young one. She's twenty-one today. Thought you'd like to sign it. You already have haven't you, Mag?

Mag *nods.*

Omar Lovely idea. (*He signs it.*) Twenty-one – what an age. To be twenty-one again . . . in 1953 I hadn't even had my first film role . . . She's a sweet girl. Give her this too. Present.

He takes the envelope from the drawer and writes on the front of it 'Love Omar' and hands it and the card back to **Daphne**.

Daphne Rightie oh.

She goes to leave.

Omar Any sign of –

Daphne Not yet. But he's bound to be late isn't he? Make an entrance . . .

Omar On a camel if he could.

Daphne I'll be back shortly – (*to* **Mag**.) Don't exhaust him with notes. (*To* **Omar**.) Then I'll give those temples a rub. (*To* **Mag**.) He likes me to do that before curtain-up sometimes.

She goes.

Omar Don't forget my UNDERPANTS.

But **Daphne** *has already gone. He sighs.*

Omar The indignity. I bet Alec Guinness never has to beg for his knickers. (*A beat.*) He's done another of those *Star Wars* films, you know, says he can't stand the fame, liar.

Tannoy Please could a member of wardrobe come to the stage. Please could a member of wardrobe come to the stage. The Grand Duchess has a hat situation.

Mag (*indicating semi-dressed woman on the envelope*) Don't you find it disturbing that they do this?

Omar Oh that's nothing. You should hear what they write. Open it. Go on.

She can't bring herself to.

Mag No. I can't.

Omar Then I will.

He picks one up and opens it reading:

'My dear Omar, I hope I can call you Omar. I feel like I know you so intimately even though we have never met in person. I've –'

Mag Stop, it's – deranged.

Omar Is it? If I can give people a bit of escape, a bit of magic, well –

A beat.

Mag Do you actually open all of it –?

Omar I usually get my housekeeper to do it. They all want something . . . It can be draining . . . Do you watch this *Star Wars*?

Mag No.

Omar Oh good. Why not?

Mag It's just glorified cowboys and Indians in space. I mean I thought Leia was an interesting character until they put her in a bikini. (*She catches herself.*) The lines. Shall we get this over with?

Omar Get this over with?

A beat.

Most people would kill to be in my company.

Mag Lines.

Omar Your wish is my command – so (*he clears his throat*): 'My dear, wouldn't you be more comfortable on the sofa? You could put your feet up there and rest.'

He is doing his make-up as he talks.

Mag 'I think I'll stay here thank you.'

Omar 'Very well just as you please . . . My dear it was so good of you to come and see me tonight.'

He considers for a moment looking at her and then puts an arm around her waist.

Mag 'You said that.'

A beat.

She removes his hand.

Omar That's in the script. (*Indicating the hand around waist and putting it back while still applying make-up with the other hand.*) 'Did I? That is a beautiful dress.'

Mag 'You said that before too.'

Omar 'What does it matter? What are words? What are words where deeds can say so much more?'

He leans towards her going in for the kiss and she elbows him hard in the stomach.

Omar Ow! That wasn't necessary – the lean-in is in the script.

Mag Yes. So's the elbow. 'Say that's just terrible.'

Omar 'What is terrible?'

Mag 'That performance of yours.' Hm.

Omar 'I fear I do not altogether understand you, Miss Dagenham.' Miss Mag are we in the play still?

Mag Yes – of course.

Omar What was that 'Hm' then?

Mag What –?

Omar 'That performance of yours.' Hm – you said. As though. It's ironic. Art imitating life. The other way?

Mag No no. I think *you* are good. Honestly.

Omar Then what? The play?

A beat.

Mag Audiences seem to love it.

Omar I didn't ask about audiences. I asked about you. What do *you* think of it?

Mag Does it matter?

Omar You are the assistant director after all . . . Do you find it funny?

Mag It is billed as a 'comedy'.

Omar Avoiding the question . . . Come on. Be brave. Tell me the truth – no one ever does. Oh to actually know what people think. No one ever tells you when you are Omar Sharif. Be the first, Mag. Go on. I dare you . . .

Mag It's not really . . . to my . . . taste.

Omar Elaborate.

Mag On the surface it's a comedy about a prince wooing a showgirl . . .

Omar Yes?

Mag But it's really about a woman being prostituted to a man in a powerful position – and that reinforces a, well, a patriarchal narrative in a pretty sinister way, by making the audience laugh at it. At her.

Omar It's just a bit of fun.

Mag It's the seediest story ever but men keep writing it – Bernard Shaw did it with *Pygmalian* too. *Gigi*, *Sabrina*, *My Fair Lady* –

Omar Eliza Doolittle is not a prostitute.

Mag She may as well be.

Omar And neither is Mary in this. She is an actress. It is a satire. We think she is a beautiful but brainless woman.

Mag And so does he. Your character. The Prince.

Omar Yes. He does. But it's not true – in the end she gets the better of him. Solves all his problems.

Mag And falls for him. Despite everything.

Omar What 'everything'?

Mag That he is shallow, puffed up and past his sell-by date.

Omar He's not old. And anyway she turns him down.

Mag At the start.

Omar She comes round because of his looks – his charm – that's why they cast me.

A beat.

But your face is telling a different story. Go on. What's your problem?

Mag He holds all the power. So what we have is people laughing at this scenario where a powerful man tries to force a woman into his bed. Not very funny in my opinion.

Omar Oh to be young again when everything was so black and white. That's your angle – but, my dear Mag, this play is a product of its time – and so you have to forgive it.

A beat.

Mag A product of its time.

Omar Why would you accept the role of assistant director if you object to the play so?

Mag Jobs in theatre are hard to come by. (*A beat.*) I'm curious as to why you would accept this role?

Omar It was good enough for Larry Olivier . . .

A beat.

Mag I suppose this is what people think of when they imagine British theatre.

Omar What do you mean?

Mag Well – posh costumes and shiny sets. Royalty on stage. Artifice. Pomp. But theatre should be much more. It can get inside you – make you think. It can change a person's mind – the way they look at the world. That's why I love it! Not this – I'm talking about Brecht. Beckett!

Omar Lovely man

Mag Samuel Beckett?

Omar We used to eat together in Paris sometimes.

Mag You're joking!

Omar I'm not – I've shared *moules* with the man. One of the kindest people I've ever met. Generous too. I tried to convince him to write a play for me. I've spent time with kings and queens, actors and directors, but I find playwrights to be the most fascinating people.

A beat.

You're impressed! I've impressed you! Don't deny it. You're looking at me differently.

A beat.

Stick with me, *hyati*, you never know who you might meet.

He is about to put some black make-up on his moustache, Daphne *enters.*

Daphne Stop! HALT!

They both look at **Daphne**. **Omar***'s make-up brush is close to his face.*

Daphne *Arrêtez*! *Pare*! *Fermare*!

Omar I understood the English!

Daphne Give me that brush.

Omar I'm using it.

Daphne Put it down.

Omar But I'm about to –

Daphne I must insist.

Through the relay we hear the cast practise for the revue later that night.

A heavy beat.

Daphne There's been a complaint.

Omar WHAT? FROM WHO?

Daphne (*a beat*) The . . . laundry. This black stuff's impossible to get out.

Omar LIES. It's not the laundry at all is it? It's her. Tell the truth, Daphne.

Daphne Well . . . Alright – I mean I don't know why I'm forced to tell you such things – surely it's the director – or ASSISTANT director's job (*looking at* **Mag**) but – yes she's made a comment about it – your moustache.

Omar What's wrong with my moustache? It's my moustache for God's sake – Omar Sharif's moustache. It's more famous than I am . . . it's more famous than she will ever be – and what's more I can have it any colour I goddamn want!

Daphne Yes of course you can, Mr Sharif, sir.

Omar What's it to her? I don't talk about her hair – or her nose – eyes – legs – or those . . . (*indicating large*) pneumatic, heaving breasts of hers – why can't she leave my moustache alone?

Daphne I understand. Only. There's the kiss. And it's leaving a mark on her – (*indicates top lip*)

A beat.

Daphne Please, Mr Sharif. Time's ticking. It's almost 7 and I've still got to help stick those jewels back onto the Grand Duchess's hat, and finish retouching the shoes.

A beat.

You'd be doing me a great favour.

A beat.

Omar Oh for Christ's sake WHO is the STAR around here anyway?

Daphne I'm just trying to keep the peace . . .

Omar Fine. Here.

He hands her the brush.

Daphne Thank you. You're very good. Temples?

He shakes his head, frustrated.

Daphne Maybe later then. Mag they're looking for you, you know – the rest of the company.

Mag I'm busy. I'll go when I'm ready.

Omar I need her. Shut the door on your way out, all that noise is giving me a headache.

Daphne *goes and shuts the door behind her.*

Omar (*shouting*) AND I NEED MY UNDERWEAR! (*To himself.*) They all stick together, these women. (*To* **Mag**.) WHAT? What are you looking at?

He finds another applicator to apply the black make-up to his moustache.

Mag *hums the tune the company are practising.*

Omar Stop. I told you it's grating. Not even in the play.

Mag It's for the revue after curtain-down tomorrow – in the tent.

Omar I know. I hate that yellow and white monstrosity.

Mag When I arrived I thought the tent was just a special touch to let the whole of Sussex know the world's most famous Arab is in residence.

Omar *gives her a wry look.*

Omar 'World's most famous Arab!' Be careful I might start thinking you are impressed . . .

A beat.

Mag Not me. My mum's watched all your films though.

They look at each other.

Omar Your MUM?

Pause.

Mag Don't you find it annoying how she keeps coming in?

Omar You're changing the subject.

Mag Daphne I mean, she never gives you a moment of privacy, isn't it maddening? She's obsessed with you, trying to get rid of me so you can both be alone.

Omar You get used to it. The adulation. At first it's annoying. Then you hardly notice it. But when it's gone – you miss it.

Mag The attention?

Omar The love.

Mag Love?

Tannoy Please could Mr Moffat and Ms Arnold come to the stage for a run of Act One, Scene One, that's Mr Moffat and Ms Arnold to the stage. Thank you.

Mag I better go and oversee that.

She makes for the door.

Omar They'll manage. I still need you.

Mag You've got the lines. You'll be fine. I'm in charge of the show, I need to –

Omar I WANT TO RUN THEM AGAIN I SAID!

A beat.

She is taken aback.

Omar I need you –

A beat.

Peter wouldn't like to hear you're mistreating the star.

A beat.

Mag Hardly mistre–

Omar O'Toole is in tonight I don't want him thinking I'm –

Mag Peter O'Toole?

Omar Florence of Arabia himself. So.

Mag And you're nervous?

Omar I didn't say that –

A beat.

Mag Let's look over Act Two, Scene Two then. (*She is flicking through her script.*) Where is it – the bit about the fault of his upbringing and then he starts downing the booze here where she says, 'You don't want to spoil my illusions of you do you?'

Omar 'What are your illusions of me?'

Mag Oh no that's not the bit – Mary's got a big speech then it must be later –

Omar Really, Mag – what are your illusions of me?

Mag Huh?

Omar I'm interested in your notes . . .

Mag My notes? Why would you take notes from me when you didn't like getting notes in rehear–

She stops herself.

Omar What are you talking about?

A beat.

Come on, be honest, no one is ever honest with me.

Mag Um. Well . . . it's just – I observed – in the rehearsal room – that Peter stopped giving you your notes publicly – after the first day. I'm guessing you asked him to stop.

Omar Of course. But that was about respect. I'm the lead. They're all looking at me. This is the first play I've done in the UK. Every interview I've done with the English press they've asked me about girlfriends and horses and gambling – nothing about the play, or my career. They're coming to see whether or not I can REALLY act. Hoping I can't – knives out.

Mag Then why are you doing it? To prove it to – [O'Toole]

Omar No. Not that. And not for the money if that's what you're thinking – my wages don't even cover the rent of the cottage . . . but the theatre is the place where an actor realises his potential most completely.

Mag You love theatre then too? Despite all the films?

Omar Of course. The stage is where an actor's presence counts. Facing his audience it's stage presence alone that wins or loses.

Mag Wins or loses.

Omar It's like a dance on stage. The audience is your partner.

He takes her into his arms and the sweeping theme music from Lawrence of Arabia *flows in as they begin to dance a waltz.*

Omar At first you are both awkward . . .

Mag I can't dance.

Omar You have to let the man lead . . . and like the audience – slowly you begin to understand, speak the same language, and work in harmony. (*They are close, moving more fluidly.*) That's it, very good. You're a fast learner . . . You all want to be whisked off your feet deep down . . . tell me the truth . . . you're a fan of *Zhivago* aren't you? What's it like to meet the doctor in person?

They are whirling around the room in a Viennese waltz as the theme tune swells. Suddenly **Daphne** *opens the door, the theme music cuts out and* **Mag** *springs away from him. She's out of breath.*

Mag We're running lines.

Daphne Which scene has dancing in it?

She's eyeing **Mag** *who is flustered and annoyed.*

Mag Don't you have some trousers to press or something?

A beat.

Daphne (*to* **Omar**) Julie asked me to come and get you.

Omar Julie?

Daphne John Gale's secretary.

Omar Why didn't she come herself?

Daphne (*impression*) 'I couldn't . . . *his* room . . . the power – the mystery . . .'

Omar That's rather a good impression, Daphne. What are you doing as a dresser when you should be on stage yourself – shouldn't she, Mag?

Daphne Well – coming from you . . . I'm – . I was thinking of doing a turn in the revue. Some of the other dressers have put a band together. They're called Bash's Backstage Boogie Band.

Omar You should join.

Daphne They've already filled the spots.

Omar What a shame. Would you like me to have a word?

Daphne You'd do that – for me?

Omar Of course. If you do something for me.

Daphne Your pants? They're nearly –

Omar No. Tell me what John wants? John Gale? You said his secretary asked you to send me up. So? What's it about?

Daphne I don't know.

Omar *approaches.*

Omar You're a terrible liar.

Daphne I'm sure it will only take a moment . . . please, Mr Sharif . . .

Omar I'll go if you give me a tiny clue what it's about . . .

Daphne I'm not supposed to know.

Omar But you do. You are the eyes and ears of the place, Daphne. You know everything don't you? Ever watchful, anticipating problems, making sure everything runs smoothly. All the buttons are in place and the hems secure. We are all in your debt . . .

Daphne Oh thank you, Mr Sharif. No one ever notices but you.

Omar So go on – tell me what you know . . . or do I need to beat it out of you?

He's flirting. **Daphne** *likes it.*

Daphne Well. It's about your pay.

Omar What about it?

Daphne Mr Gale's a teeny bit upset you told the rest of the company what you're earning.

Mag You're getting more?

Omar I wouldn't be so unchivalrous as to brag about it.

Daphne No. Of course not. But the stage manager found out. And seems to have been . . . indiscreet . . .

Omar How would he know?

Daphne You gifted the ASM – the birthday girl – your wages . . . remember?

Omar Oh . . . yes.

Daphne And she's been blabbing to anyone who'll listen.

Mag You mean that envelope you gave Daphne earlier was your pay packet?

Omar It's her twenty-first birthday. Only happens once. Twenty-one!

Mag How much was in it?

Omar All of it.

Mag You gave her a week's wages. As a birthday present? HOW MUCH?

Omar £750. I didn't think she'd tell everyone.

Mag What's everyone else getting?

Daphne The top salary's normally £500.

Mag There'll be a mutiny!

Daphne (*to* **Mag**) Mr Gale hit the roof.

Mag I bet he did.

Omar I was TRYING to do something nice, it's called GENEROSITY!

Daphne Well, you'd better run along and tell Mr Gale that –

Omar RUN ALONG? WHY WHY DO I HAVE TO GO TO HIM? I'm not at his beck and call – HE IS AT MINE. THIS ENGLISH behaviour – ENGLISH people – *QUE SUMAK*!

Daphne Mr Sharif – please calm –

Omar I WILL NOT CALM DOWN. It's an insult – a BLOODY INSULT – questioning my – motives! You people may not understand the concept of GENEROSITY but where I come from we are GENEROUS. Give GIFTS – with no motive. TELL HIM THAT.

He walks towards **Daphne** *and she backs out the door.*

Omar TELL HIM TO HAVE SOME BLOODY RESPECT – SUMMONING ME!

He slams the door.

I'm not a fucking JINNI! [genie]

He is furious. Kicks something.

He kicks something else. Tears something up.

Omar *Il an abouki*! English English English FUCKERS! These people! Fuck them all! Presuming the worst, some ulterior motive! I will NEVER understand this place. They think they are better than everyone else!

He is almost hyperventilating and shaking. At first it seems like rage. But then it starts to look like vulnerability.

Mag Yes. They do.

Omar WHY WHY WHY WHY WHY DO THEY DO THIS!

He is shaking. She approaches – shocked at the violence of his physical reaction.

Omar WHY, Mag?

Mag It's ok.

She puts her hands on his arms to stop him shaking and sits him down.

Omar England is another country. Another planet. I knew that from when I came here as a boy.

She lights a cigarette and hands it to him. As he smokes he calms.

Omar Thank you. (*A beat.*) But I can deal with them. With all of it. I can. I'm adaptable. And a gentleman fits in anywhere . . .

A beat.

Mag A sponge fits in anywhere.

A beat.

He looks at her hard.

Omar That's from *Funny Girl*. (*A beat.*) So it's not just your mother who watches my movies?

Mag *frowns.*

Omar When you frown like that. It's familiar . . . my son, he has the same forehead crease.

A beat.

I don't like liars, subterfuge, if you have something to say, say it!

Tannoy Ladies and gentlemen of the *Sleeping Prince* company this is your half-hour call. 30 minutes please.

A beat.

Omar You know my films . . .

Mag Everyone knows your films.

Omar What exactly do you want? Did someone send you here to watch me? Mr Gale? Tell me the truth!

Tannoy Good evening, ladies and gentlemen, and welcome to the Festival Theatre. This evening's performance of *The Sleeping Prince* will begin at 7.30 p.m.

Omar *hits the tannoy in annoyance.*

Mag I'm just here to give you notes. And now I have I'll go.

She walks to the door.

Omar NO YOU GO WHEN I SAY YOU CAN GO. WE AREN'T FINISHED. I DECIDE.

Mag'*s hand is on the handle.*

Omar What if I refused to perform tonight – then what? You could lose your job.

A beat.

And I bet spying work is hard to come by.

Mag I'm not a spy! I'm actually on your side. I see the things you see – I understand what it's like to have to deal with people like that every day, people who make presumptions who never actually take the time to listen or – (*She stops herself.*)

Pause.

He regards her.

Omar You know – a woman in California once came to my room with a gun. She wanted to – well she wanted me to . . . make love to her. This is the problem with Americans – they think guns are the answer to everything. She made me take off all my clothes and she lay on top of me but you know that kind of pressure can give one . . . stage fright. The woman got very angry. She said I'd made a living from the image of the great lover and it was all false.

Mag Why are you telling me this?

Omar By way of clumsy apology. (*A beat.*) Sometimes it can be hard to trust people.

A beat.

Mag Will you get in trouble? For revealing your wages?

Omar Oh, *hyati*. No. What's he going to do – sack me? Besides – between you and me, the theatre has just lost their Martini sponsorship, they need me now more than ever.

Mag You can't say that to him!

Omar No. I have tact. I'll tell him that they'd be more shocked if I was earning the same as them. I'm a Hollywood star.

Mag You think we'll be talking about having done this play with you for the rest of our lives.

Omar You will.

Mag And that makes you happy.

He looks in the mirror, smooths out the lines on his forehead.

Omar Yes. Everyone wants to be remembered. It'll be my generosity you remember I expect. Ten years ago it would have been my face – my smile, intense stare. But now –

Mag It's the same face. It's – [*handsome*]

She wipes something from his shoulder.

Omar That's dust –

A beat.

Mag You keep calling me *hyati*.

Omar It means darling in Arabic.

Mag *Hyati* . . .

There's a gentle knock and **Daphne** *enters with some papers.*

Daphne Did you hear, Mr Sharif, that's the half?

Omar I heard.

Daphne I'm sorry about that. Don't worry – Mr Gale was trying to come in but I sent him away, said you were too busy.

Omar Thank you for protecting me.

Daphne It's nothing – you are the kindest – we've had all sorts in that chair in my time – Joan Collins, Tom Baker,

Peter Bowles, Penelope Wilton, Derek Jacobi all perfectly pleasant but none as thoughtful as you . . . you always notice us behind-the-scene types and that's appreciated . . . listen to me blathering on now. Here are the press cuttings you asked for.

Omar Thank you. My mother likes to read them all.

Daphne You need some quiet time. Shall I rub your temples?

Omar No. Mag and I are still busy. You can go. Thank you.

Daphne *looks put out but goes.*

He vigorously brushes the 'dust' from his shoulders as **Mag** *picks up the reviews.*

Mag You're not really sending these to your mother?

Omar Why not?

Mag They're not exactly –

Omar She likes to see them –

Mag 'Sleepwalking through the role' you can't be pleased with that.

Omar Mr Morley is entitled to his opinion. Listen: 'You could almost hear the ladies sigh as the heart-throb hero of *Doctor Zhivago* stepped on stage for the first time in 25 years. If he was nervous it did not show. Sharif of the warm brown eyes was subtle and succinct, compelling and capable in a role that honestly is not a great one. If anything he was too handsome, too charming for the character Rattigan intended.' You see!

Mag Oh that's just the local rag. (*She picks up another.*) 'Omar Sharif as the Grand Duke won the house over simply by being a film star. He plays very pleasantly but without any great magnetism.' Doesn't it bother you?

Omar I'm no fool. Theatre is elitist – full of snobs who don't want a film actor coming and polluting this sacrosanct place . . .

Mag What if the bad reviews –

Omar Mixed not bad.

Mag Mixed reviews aren't about you being a star?

Omar You mean that, like you, they dislike the play?

Mag Oh God no. They *adore* Rattigan. No I mean what if they dislike you in this role for another reason?

Omar Go on.

A beat.

Directors need balls, remember?

Mag In the same way that they all went mad when they saw an Arab kissing a white woman in *Funny Girl* – they don't like you pawing their young white virginal beauty here . . . (*She indicates* Othello *text.*) "A black ram tupping their white ewe."

Omar The issue with *Funny Girl* was quite different. That was about Barbra being Jewish as much as it was about me being an Arab. And what you are probably too young to realise is there was also a war on –

Mag The Six-Day War also known as the third Arab–Israeli war which was between the 5 and 10 of June 1967 and saw Israel take up arms against Egypt, Syria and Jordan, it was claimed to be as a result of Nasser closing the Straits of Tiran to Israeli shipping but of course it was a conflict whose seeds had been planted with the creation of the state of Israel in 1948 after the British were kicked out of mandated Palestine by the growing Jewish immigrant population in the wake of the Holocaust and the Second World War.

Omar (*impressed*) I'm surprised they teach it in schools here.

Mag They don't.

A beat.

Omar You think I got mixed reviews because I'm an Arab?

Mag Precisely.

Omar But none of them mentioned that.

Mag They didn't have to. It's all subliminal. Subtextual. About how you look. How *Arab* you look.

Omar I doubt it.

Mag Doesn't the *possibility* bother you?

Omar Not really. As Mr Billington says: 'It's tomorrow's fish and chip paper.'

Mag No. Language matters. Insinuation. Inference. It burrows inside the reader's head and festers there. Poisons. Infects. Makes things they think privately actually begin to seem acceptable . . . and slowly gives licence for any Tom, Dick or Harry to call someone a towel head. And worse. It makes it ok for them to hurt – punch – kick. KILL.

Omar That's quite a leap . . .

Mag One so-called journalist called you a sandboy!

Omar That just means I'm happy.

Mag They could have said happy!

A beat.

Omar I'm afraid you are forcing the facts to fit your thesis. They don't resent me for my 'Orientalness'.

Mag No. What then?

No answer.

Mag What else could –

Omar HOW SHOULD I KNOW?

A beat.

Mag You seem annoyed. I think you know I'm right.

Omar No, madam, black and white you are not. It's nothing to do with where I'm from, it's about something you wouldn't even consider.

Mag Try me.

Omar Age, my dear, age.

Mag But you're –

Omar Getting older. Heart-throbs aren't supposed to you see – they should remain forever young. The older I get the older they get and they don't like seeing me ageing just as they do. They called me solid, stiff, ageing, grey-haired. That's what they are annoyed about . . . but I am still attractive. I'm still a bankable star, aren't I? They come to see Omar Sharif – they want me don't they? Even little English girls like you look at me a certain way . . .

A beat.

Mag Who said I'm English?

He looks at her questioningly.

Omar Go on.

Mag My mum's Scottish.

A beat.

And. Your father?

A beat.

Mag Foreign.

A beat.

They look at each other. **Mag** *is embarrassed.*

Omar So where in the Arab world is your father from then? I presume that's the foreign you refer to?

No answer.

Ib-Tehki Arabeey?

Mag *winces slightly.*

Omar You don't look Arab – you don't speak Arabic. (*A beat.*) I knew you were hiding something.

Mag I don't know why I even brought it up. It's not even – [relevant]

Omar Do you claim to be an Arab?

A beat.

Mag My father was an Arab. So – I am half-Arabic.

He turns away from her. She is longing to know his reaction.

Pause.

Omar I wouldn't go around telling people that. They won't understand it. And you'd never know.

She is thrown.

Mag I don't – tell people. Usually.

Pause.

Omar I need to get dressed now. You can go.

Mag What?

Omar I need to get dressed.

Daphne *opens the door.*

Daphne Are you not dressed yet?

Omar You again. Why didn't you knock? Always listening at doors! I am not a child. What do you want?

Daphne Please forgive me, Mr Sharif. I just came to tell you Mr O'Toole's not here yet.

Omar Is that it?

Daphne No, and to see if Frankie's roller boot is here – she's lost one.

Omar Yes. I nearly tripped over it and broke my leg. Then what would happen? No one wants to see the understudy.

Mag *picks up the roller boot.*

Mag Is this what you're looking for?

Daphne *takes it but doesn't engage or look at* **Mag***; she is still annoyed with how she spoke to her before.*

Omar Why didn't Frankie come and get it herself?

Daphne *turns up the relay and we hear Frankie singing in the auditorium.*

Daphne Listen – she's warming up, see . . .

On the tannoy Frankie sings. It's sassy and brilliant.

Daphne *is humming along.* **Omar** *is annoyed.*

Omar You've musical leanings too, Daphne?

Daphne Well, no. Not really.

Omar You said yourself you wanted to sing in the revue – so let's hear you. Entertain us.

Daphne I couldn't.

Omar Why not? This is a wonderful opportunity. An assistant – sorry, a *director* and me. Go on – impress us.

Daphne *looks embarrassed.*

Omar SING!

A beat.

Omar Sing what she's singing. (*Indicating the relay.*)

Daphne I don't know it.

Omar *turns down the relay and looks at* **Daphne** *expectantly. She is mortified.*

Omar You were just singing along. Go on.

A beat.

This could be your big moment . . . like in the movies. Dresser to star!

A beat.

Daphne *looks pleadingly at* **Mag** *for support.* **Mag** *looks away.*

Omar COME ON, DAPHNE, WE HAVEN'T GOT ALL DAY. SING, WOMAN!

It takes a moment and then suddenly the music fills the space – it is as if we are in a musical she sings with gusto the same song Frankie sung, and tap dances with **Omar** *joining in.*

Suddenly the dream is over.

Omar STOP STOP STOP, THAT IS AWFUL!

Daphne *runs from the room.*

A beat.

Mag *is looking at him annoyed. He turns from her.*

Omar You can go too.

Mag She's not a performing monkey.

Omar I didn't *make* her do anything.

Mag You humiliated her.

Omar Then why didn't you stop me?

A beat.

Because you dislike Daphne, you think you are better than her.

Mag This – it isn't about me –

Omar You, my Mag, are a hypocrite. I didn't make her sing. I encouraged her.

Mag You scared her.

Omar I what? What are you talking about – she rubs my temples every night. Makes my warm-up gargle.

A beat.

Now, this has all been very interesting. We can talk more at dinner, later.

A beat.

You can go. Send Daphne back in.

A beat.

Mag Five minutes ago you were practically barring the door, now you can't wait to be shot of me. What's changed? You've got ethics about flirting with an Arab girl?

Omar Don't be ridiculous, you're young enough to be my daughter.

Mag Is that it? Worried I'm your progeny? The product of some forgettable one-night stand? And that this is all getting a bit Greek?

A beat.

Omar No. You're not mine.

Mag Are you sure?

Omar I only have one child. A boy.

Mag So what's changed?

Omar Now I know you want something from me. British always think you want something. Arabs always do.

Mag But you've been offering!

Omar Offering and being asked are two different things. One is graceful, the other vulgar. Do you know how often I am solicited for help, begged to do things for others, give them money? And the most irritating thing is I *would* have offered. But once they ask. Well, it's – distasteful.

Mag I don't want anything!

Omar Everyone wants something.

Tannoy Ladies and gentlemen of *The Sleeping Prince* company, the house is now open so please do not cross the stage. This is also your quarter-hour call, you have 15 minutes please, 15 minutes, thank you.

A beat.

Mag How about a game of backgammon?

He turns his back on her silently, dismissing her.

Omar They've called the quarter.

Mag You're not on until page 8, there's time.

She's not going anywhere.

We could make it more interesting . . .

A beat.

Omar I told you – I don't bet against people with purple sweaters.

Mag I'm not proposing we bet money. But if you win I'll give you what you want . . . you say no one tells you the truth? Well, now's your chance to find out what people really think of you. I'll tell you.

Omar Interesting. And if I lose? What's the stake?

Mag You have to do something for me. I'll think of something I want.

No answer.

But if you'd rather have Daphne's sycophantic fawning over you than a robust conversation and a good game – for fun.

Omar Fine, but if we play you answer all of my questions – about you. Tell me everything I want to know. (*A beat.*) A fact or an item of clothing.

Mag Really? What the hell. Ok.

She gets the board.

White or brown?

Omar It's all the same to me.

Mag *sets up the game.*

Omar This is one of the oldest games in existence. Originated in Mesopotamia five thousand years ago. Modern-day Iraq.

A beat.

They begin to play.

Omar Is your father Iraqi?

Mag No.

Omar I thought you were going to answer my questions? Otherwise (*Indicates taking off clothes.*)

Mag Fine. He's not Iraqi, he's Lebanese.

Omar Ah. Hence the knowledge about the Six-Day War. Do I remind you of him?

Mag He's darker. But he had the moustache. He shaved it once. Because I begged him to. But he looked awful. I didn't realise he had no top lip at all. It really scared me, he was like a different person.

Omar Why did you want him to shave it?

Mag I don't know.

Omar Yes you do.

Mag I didn't like it.

Omar Lying. Take something off.

Mag *takes off her shoes.*

Omar Disappointing. Nevertheless. I'll ask again – why did you want him to shave it, *hyati*?

Mag *Hyati* again.

Omar You prefer *habibti*?

Mag *looks blank.*

Omar Another way of saying darling. What did your father teach you?

A beat.

And why did you want him to shave?

A beat.

You can tell me . . .

Mag It's silly – there'd been this – incident.

Omar What incident?

Mag I told you it's silly – I don't want to talk about it.

Omar Then take off something else.

A beat.

She looks at him.

Omar I think you do want to tell me.

A beat.

Mag He'd been using a phone box and I was waiting outside – I must have been eight or nine. And this white – English guy came and started banging on the window because he needed to use the phone. And he started shouting, 'HURRY UP, HURRY UP, YOU FUCKING' – I don't want to say it. You know what he said. An awful word. He'd never been called that before. And he was so angry he shook. I had to hold his arms. Give him a cigarette to calm him down.

She looks to him for a reaction.

Omar Ah. So you wanted him to shave it so people wouldn't identify him as different.

Mag I suppose.

Omar You thought with no moustache he would look less Arab.

Mag God. It sounds so –

Omar Even though it was actually his skin colour that set him apart.

A beat.

Mag I watched. Silently.

Omar Like St Peter.

Mag I don't know what that means.

Omar Peter was a traitor – he betrayed Christ. You feel like you betrayed your father and who you are.

Mag Yes. I suppose.

A beat.

She's searching his face trying to read his thoughts.

Mag Has anything like that ever happened to you?

Omar Of course not. I'm not a Paki.

Mag What?

She is stunned. It's as though he hit her.

Mag What did you say?

It's as though the temperature has dropped. **Mag** *cannot rip her eyes from him. It's like she's seeing him for the first time.*

Tannoy Ladies and gentlemen of *The Sleeping Prince* company, this is your five minute call you have five minutes please, five minutes.

Daphne *is at the door again. She looks a little sheepish, and is embarrassed and formal. She has a glass of liquid.*

Omar Ah. Daphne.

Daphne Mr Sharif. It's almost time. I've got your special gargle.

We begin to hear the audience entering the theatre.

Omar Leave it on the side. I'm just – teaching this one a thing or two that's all.

Daphne Are you – *completely* ready?

Omar Oh – you mean my – (*indicates pants*) no. They never arrived so you'd better warn the dressers.

Daphne For goodness' sake – I sent the birthday girl with them – I'll go and see what happened –

Omar Thank you, Daphne . . . I hope you know . . . how much I appreciate . . .

A beat.

He takes a faded flower from the vase and hands it to her.

Daphne Oh . . . Thank you – Mr Sharif . . .

She goes to leave but turns back.

Mr Sharif . . . before I go – you must permit me to . . .

Omar What?

Daphne May I – touch – your – moustache?

Omar Touch my –?

Daphne *She* doesn't believe you won't have make-up on it. I've been asked to test it.

Omar Oh for God's sake.

Daphne Please, Mr Sharif. Just prove to me it's *au natural* and I'll go and fetch your pants and we can get on with the show. Until then they're holding the curtain.

A beat.

She always gets a laugh after the kiss. Because of the mark you leave on her face. I've never liked it, that's when they start to warm to her. The audience. Isn't that what they call upstaging? To be honest, I've always though that it distracts from your wonderful performance.

A beat.

Daphne *tentatively leans towards him unsure whether* **Mag** *has convinced him enough to let her touch his moustache. It's as though she's approaching a wild animal. He permits her to touch it. Then she examines her fingers – they are black. She shows them to him unimpressed.*

Omar It must be from before . . .

She proceeds to wipe it off with a tissue as if he is a child.

Daphne Thank you, Mr Sharif. We must all do things that are beneath us sometimes . . . now I'll go and see where your knickers have got to.

She looks at the black tissue disgusted and then puts it in the bin before leaving.

A beat.

Omar *frowns, then reapplies his moustache.*

Omar One night in Italy I won a million dollars you know – that was probably my best night. It's a good story. I wasn't planning on going to the casino. I'd been in the discotheque dancing with a beautiful girl all night and at the end of the evening I invited her to my room but she refused. I was surprised. And rather annoyed, so I went to the casino instead. And luck was on my side. Imagine. A million dollars in a night. I sent a truck of roses to the girl the next day to thank her for not coming to my room.

Mag *rolls and they return to the backgammon in silence. After a few moves.*

Omar Oh. That was mean.

They play a little more.

Omar I've got you now.

She throws.

Omar Lucky.

They play more.

Omar Avoiding blots. No candlesticks. You aren't a novice are you? I hope you aren't hustling me, young lady . . .

They play a little more.

Another knock on the door. **Daphne** *enters with* **Omar***'s freshly laundered undies.*

Tannoy Ladies and gentlemen of *The Sleeping Prince* company, this is your Act One beginners call. Act One beginners to the stage please: Miss Arnold and Mr Moffet. Stand by please, stage management and technical staff. Thank you.

Daphne Here you are, Mr Sharif. In the nick of time.

Omar What happened to them – why didn't the birthday girl deliver them?

Daphne She . . . didn't want to . . .

Omar Why not? Why wouldn't she want to come and see me?

A look passes between **Mag** *and* **Daphne**.

Daphne The gift. Your gift. To her. You have to understand that in England –

Omar THAT MONEY was a birthday present! That's all! What is wrong with the English?!

Daphne No no, don't misunderstand – she's – *star-struck.*

A beat.

No one believes her.

Omar They better not be damp. I will not wear them if they are damp.

Daphne They're still toasty from the radiator. (*A beat.*) The house is open.

Omar And?

Daphne He's not here yet. Are you sure it was today?

Omar OF COURSE I'M SURE!

Daphne Don't forget your gargle.

She exits.

Omar *puts on his pants.*

Omar Uncomfortable bloody things. Is it my go?

He rolls and moves. Then **Mag** *rolls and blocks him.*

Omar A hit! You are good. Aggressive play. But I am the king of comebacks see? Now we can finish after the show –

Mag *gets up and closes the door, standing in front of it.*

Mag I'm not done yet.

A beat.

He goes to leave but she blocks him.

Omar What's the matter?

Mag I thought I liked you but – what you said before about not being a – I can't say that word – you know – What the FUCK?

Omar Well, I'm not.

Mag That's it? That's all you've got to say.

Omar I don't have time for histrionics.

Mag No solidarity – no empathy? CHRIST!

Omar Move. Or I'll move you.

Mag Go on then. I dare you.

He looks at her.

Mag Are you going to do to me what you did to that woman?

Omar Which woman?

Mag The one who came to your party. Who was always at the stage door. But she wasn't the fan you thought she was, was she? Just a nutter and she annoyed you but wouldn't leave, so you slammed her face into a wall. That's what everyone is talking about–

Omar STOP – STOP /

Mag / how she bled all over your party.

Omar You're better than this – hearsay and gossip – you've just spent time with me. Got to know me! She walked into that wall. Drunk.

Mag You wanted the truth, well, that's why they're all scared of you! What would the press say? What would Mr Gale say? What would your fans say?

Omar I don't have to explain myself to you – but . . . it's not true. Yes I have a temper but I have never hurt anyone intentionally.

Mag And if you did you'd send flowers as an apology. So that makes everything ok.

A beat.

He tries to get past her – they are close.

Omar Your anger is not for me.

Tannoy Mr Sharif, this is your call to the stage please, Mr Sharif, your call to the stage, thank you.

Mag *turns the key in the door to lock it and then holds it in her hand.*

Mag You are so . . . normal . . . predictable . . .

Omar Meeting a star is always disappointing. Fans think they know them, because they project all their desires and longing. How can we ever live up to that?

Mag Stars like Omar Sharif?

Omar Yes. Me.

Mag THERE IS NO OMAR SHARIF! YOUR NAME IS MICHAEL!

Omar It's true that I was christened Michael yes. That's no secret.

Mag Christened. You're Christian.

Omar By birth. I converted to get married. But you know that. You seem to know a lot about me.

Mag I've read about you – I was looking for answers, Michael. But you changed your name to Omar because why – it didn't sound exotic enough?

Omar The name Michael annoyed me. Anybody could be a Michael. I needed something catchier – something that rolled off the tongue.

Mag Something Arabic?

Omar Why not?

Mag But look at what the outcome was. You became the most famous Arab in the world. Men want to be you and women want to be with you. You've created this fantasy Oriental man, they see you on screen and they fall in love with you, and then – because they can't take *you* home they go hunting for their own brown-skinned man to take to bed.

Omar Like your mother? Which film was it? Let me guess – *Zhivago*?

Mag That's not the point!

Omar I don't see what's so bad! I once heard a Brazilian girl say the answer to the world's problems is for us to keep making love 'til we're all the same colour. You should be thanking me. It sounds like without me you might not exist.

Mag I wouldn't be this – this – mongrel as my granny called me. A half-breed. It's like there's a barrier between me and them. Between me and everyone. I'm not British. Not Lebanese. Not anything. Nothing.

Omar What are you complaining about? No one would even know you are an Arab. You could watch your father being abused and they didn't even know you were related.

Mag No. It's not, because – it's in my blood. And it's like they can all smell it. I can't get away from it.

Omar Of course you can. No one need know. Being an Arab is thornier than you suppose. Better to be English. You can choose. You're lucky.

Mag You mean pretend. Lie. Dissemble. Act. Like you do. Mr Michael Omar Christian Muslim –

Omar I never lie.

She throws the key across the room in frustration.

Mag I thought I might learn something from you. That's why I took this job . . . But you're just like everyone else. Looking for an angle as you put it. You changed your name to Omar Sharif to exploit your Arabness – I've had to – to shorten mine to sound more English. We aren't the same at all.

There is a knocking on the door.

Mag You're like this play – a product of its time, you've got nothing to teach me or anyone.

Omar You silly girl. This is not about me – it's about your father. Let me guess – he was a religious fanatic and deported.

Mag No – NO he was not – not that . . . his country is fucked up – thanks to the British and the French. He was fucked up. But he covered it. Seemed normal. He couldn't cope with life though. Here. Called all the names under the sun. Abused. Beaten up. Bled rivers. So he left. Wanted us to go with him but Mum was scared. Didn't want to leave the UK. He went back and died there. And now I'm stuck here. Cut adrift. Not this and not that. Alone. It's bad enough being a woman. And poor. But add being half-Arab – half anything – to that list and you're totally fucked.

The knocking on the door is more frantic.

Daphne (*outside*) Mr Sharif! Mag!

A beat.

Mag And for one small minute I thought you might understand. I'm such an idiot.

Tannoy Mr Sharif to the wings please, Mr Sharif to the wings.

Omar I don't have time for this. I need to go on stage.

Mag NO. I'm not finished.

A beat.

Omar You want me to teach you something? Then listen – you were sneering at these women (*indicating letters*), at Daphne, but you are the same as them – projecting your hopes and desires onto me – but I'm just a man trying to do my job. Let me go on stage.

Mag I haven't got what I want out of this yet.

He's on the floor hunting for the key.

Omar Now we get to it. Everyone wants something. What – a job? Money?

A beat.

Mag No. I want you to get it – to feel the way my dad felt. The way I feel.

Omar What do you mean?

Mag You've never felt like an outsider because you're Omar Sharif. But I want you to. To feel what that's like. To understand how these people would look at you. Talk to you. Treat you. If you were just another Arab.

A beat.

She grabs the razor from his dressing table.

Omar My razor. What are you doing with that?

A beat.

Mag I am going to use it.

Omar You want me dead?

Mag I'm not going to kill you. Or stop you going on stage. Get up. You are going out there tonight. But first (*a beat*) we are going to shave off your moustache. You said it yourself. It's more famous than you are. Without it . . . well, you're not Omar Sharif. Are you? You're just another 'towel head'.

Pause.

He rises.

Omar Are you mad? I'm not going to let you shave my moustache. I am the man here.

He knocks over the backgammon threateningly and kicks over the post bag so the letters fall over the floor.

Mag STOP IT! I'm the one with the blade. Sit down. Go on – I mean it.

She brandishes it.

Frightened O'Toole won't recognise you? That no one will?

Reluctantly **Omar** *backs down and sits.*

Mag *approaches him with caution – blade outstretched.*

Omar Your hands are shaking. Be careful. One false move and you'll end a man's life.

Mag *is nervous. He is still. They watch each other in the mirror. She brings the blade closer and closer to his face then . . .*

Tannoy Mr Sharif to the wings please. Mr Sharif to the stage. Thank you.

Omar What would your father say if he could see you now? (*He speaks in Arabic.*) *Ibnatee tatawaqaf ean altasaruf kalhuyawan watahtarim shuyukhak.* [My daughter stop behaving like an animal and respect your elders.]

Mag *looks sickened.*

Mag STOP!

Omar You understood?

Mag No.

A beat.

I hate it.

Omar The language?

Mag It's ugly. Like spitting. Hocking up and spitting.

Omar No no no – you are wrong. It's beautiful.

A beat.

Listen:

ليس فيك من قدرة على الضر بي نصف ما في من قدرة على تحمل الأذى

laysa feek min qudra 'ala d-durr bee nisf
ma feeyya min qudra 'ala taḥammul el-adha.

Mag Disgusting. PLEASE STOP!

Omar That's not disgusting – it's Emilia. From *Othello.*

'Thou hast not half that power to do me harm

As I have to be hurt.'

You're a theatre person – you can't hate Shakespeare – whatever language it is in.

A beat.

But it's not the language you hate – NO. It's the fact you can't speak it.

No answer.

I'm right aren't I?

A beat.

Omar I can teach you –

Mag You – teach me?

Omar Of course. Imagine being taught Arabic by Omar Sharif!

Mag But –

Omar It would give you a connection to your past. Your father's world. Your heritage.

A beat.

Habibti anna – give me the blade. Let me help you /

Mag What about all this?

Omar We'll forget it ever happened. You won, your prize is Arabic lessons – *khalas*. Everything else forgotten. I promise. Just give me the razor . . .

A beat.

Yulla. Habibti.

A beat.

The Lawrence of Arabia *music plays quietly. She stares at him mesmerised. Then hands over the razor as there is a key in the door – it opens and* **Daphne** *rushes in as the music cuts out.*

Daphne What's going on?

She looks unsure from one to the other.

Are you alright, Mr Sharif?

Omar Am I alright, Mag?

Mag Yes.

Daphne Are you alright, Mag?

Mag *nods.*

Omar Good. I'm going on stage. But I'll see you at the end of the show for your first lesson. OK?

Mag OK.

Daphne You really must go on, Mr Sharif.

Omar Don't fuss.

He leaves, but not before quietly approaching **Mag** *as she approached him when he was upset, and holding her arms briefly in the same way. Then he nods and leaves.*

A beat.

Daphne *and* **Mag** *stare at each other for a moment.*

Daphne *begins to tidy up the room.* **Mag** *watches for a moment. Then she turns up the relay. We hear* **Omar** *go out on stage and a huge round of applause.*

Now we hear The Sleeping Prince *over the relay from where the The Regent enters – it continues in the background.*

Daphne What was going on – why was the door locked?

No answer.

More laughing from the audience. **Daphne** *turns down the tannoy.*

A beat.

Daphne *finds the key.*

What's this key doing down here. Mag?

A beat.

Mag You've a nice voice. You should sing in the cabaret. Tonight.

Daphne Are you taking the mickey?

Mag No. I mean it. You just need more confidence.

Daphne Oh. Well. He usually wants me here after the show. Help him take off his make-up. Post-show debrief that sort of thing . . . and he'll be in a foul mood. O'Toole never turned up.

Mag I'll be here. He's going to teach me Arabic.

A beat.

Mag *turns up the tannoy. She hears the audience clapping and laughing.*

Mag *then starts tidying the letters that have spilled on the floor –* **Daphne** *picks up one with a woman's photo in her underwear on the envelope. She looks at it for a moment and then decides to open it. She reads – as she does the sweeping theme music from* Lawrence of Arabia *is back.*

Daphne 'My dear Omar, I hope I can call you Omar. I feel like I know you so intimately even though we have never met in person. I've watched every single one of your films and even some of the ones in Arabic though I don't understand them. I go as many times as I can manage – sometimes to two showings in a row. I can't stop myself because when I look into those liquid eyes on the screen I know you and only you will ever understand me. That only you can know me. The deep corners of who I really am. My name is Edith. I'm sorry it's such an ugly name. Perhaps when we meet you might find a different name for me – one that you think suits me better. Then I'd be born again – a new person, made by you.'

The sound of a record being pulled off a player and the needle scratching. **Mag** *takes the letter and puts it into the post bag hurriedly with all the other post and ties the bag as though she doesn't want anything from inside to escape.*

She stares at the post bag and then –

Daphne You should teach yourself Arabic you know.

A beat.

The two women look at each other.

Blackout.

www.ingramcontent.com/pod-product-compliance
Lightning Source LLC
LaVergne TN
LVHW052343100826
845147LV00021B/1166

9781350661622